What Makes Me Do The Things I Do?

Molly Potter

ILLUSTRATED BY
Sarah Jennings

FEATHERSTONE
LONDON OXFORD NEW YORK NEW DELHI SYDNEY

This book is dedicated to my huge-hearted, Scouse friend Elle who I will admit to having got up to a fair amount of mischief with (but we know better now obviously).

FEATHERSTONE
Bloomsbury Publishing Plc
50 Bedford Square, London, WC1B 3DP, UK
29 Earlsfort Terrace, Dublin 2, Ireland
BLOOMSBURY, FEATHERSTONE and the Feather logo are trademarks of Bloomsbury Publishing Plc
First published in Great Britain, 2022 by Bloomsbury Publishing Plc
Text copyright © Molly Potter, 2022
Illustrations copyright © Sarah Jennings, 2022

A catalogue record for this book is available from the British Library

ISBN: HB: 978-1-4729-7398-6; ePDF: 978-1-4729-7397-9; ePub 978-1-4729-7399-3

2 4 6 8 10 9 7 5 3 1

Printed and bound in China by Leo Paper Products, Heshan, Guangdong

To find out more about our authors and books visit www.bloomsbury.com and sign up for our newsletters

Dear Reader,

This is a book all about behaviour. Behaviour is what people do, what they say and how they act. We often behave in different ways depending on where we are, who we're with, how we feel and what we're thinking. Some of our behaviours can be helpful and some can make situations worse.

This book helps you think about different behaviours. It considers why you might sometimes behave in ways that are not helpful and it also looks at the ways in which positive behaviours can help you and other people. It will help you think about why we choose to act the way we do.

The thing to remember about behaviour is that we do have some control over it. No matter what we're feeling, we can usually choose how we react. This book will help you think about which behaviours you'd like to do more of and which you might want to do less of or not at all!

Contents

Telling lies...

Some children tell lies more than others. Telling a lie is not usually a good thing to do, so why might you sometimes tell lies?

To try and **get out of doing things you don't want to do.**

I can't possibly tidy my room, I've got so much homework!

To **impress** other people.

Yes, I can juggle.

So you **don't get told off.**

No, I didn't take the last bit of cake.

Because it's **easier** than telling the truth.

That's a brilliant dinosaur outfit.

...Or being honest

Being honest nearly always turns out better than telling lies. Let's look at why this is.

People will **trust** you to tell the truth.

> Is there a smudge on my face?

> Yes - it's from your pen.

Lies often get **found out** and make you look silly.

> Next week we're going on a school trip to learn circus skills.

> You'll be able to show us your juggling Lottie.

Telling the truth is **brave and admirable.**

> Did you let the dog jump on the sofa?

> Yes, sorry. I didn't realise he had muddy paws.

Being honest can be really **helpful.**

> Your costume isn't looking too good. Do you want to use this one instead?

It's good to know...
Lies that we tell to avoid hurting someone's feelings are called white lies, for instance if we said we liked someone's new coat when we didn't really. These are usually not harmful lies.

7

Not doing what you're told...

Children don't always do what adults have asked them to do. Why might this be?

You might want to **keep on doing what** you're doing.

> Time to wash up.

> But there's loads more left in the bowl!

You might **not want to do what you're being asked** to do.

> It's time to clean out your hamster's cage.

You might **not feel confident** about what you're being asked to do.

> This won't take you long to clean.

You might just feel lazy.

> Can you help me put the books away?

...Or following instructions

The adults in your life ask you to do things to keep you safe and healthy, and to encourage you to make good choices. It's a good idea to do what you're asked because...

The adult will be **really pleased** with you.

Amazing! I thought I was going to have to ask twenty times.

You probably **can't get out of** what you've been asked to do, so you might as well get on and do it.

Can I go back and play with my toys now?

You're probably being asked to do something for a **good reason.**

Put the biscuits away now or you won't want your dinner.

It's good to **help adults** when they need it and it will make you feel good too.

It's good to know...

If you're asked to keep a secret, unless it's a nice surprise for someone, check with one or two adults to see if they also think it is a good idea.

9

Losing your temper...

People lose their temper or have a tantrum when they're not getting their own way and are feeling angry. Temper tantrums can be quite powerful and not enjoyable for the person having them or for anyone else nearby. Why do people lose their temper?

Some people struggle to **control their temper** more than others.

We might think losing our temper will **get us what we want** – although it hardly ever does.

Losing our temper gets **people's attention** quickly.

We might get cross to **get out of doing something**.

...Or staying calm

Staying calm can sometimes be really difficult. But when we do, things nearly always turn out better because...

We make better decisions.

People are more likely to listen to us.

We're unlikely to get told off.

Other people react better to us.

It's good to know...

We all get angry sometimes, but it's how we react that matters. If we take a bit of time to cool down before we act, we're less likely to make the situation worse.

11

Cheating...

Cheating is when you do something that's unfair to try and get a better result. You can cheat in games by not following the rules or cheat at school work by copying someone else. Why might you be tempted to cheat?

You might be **more likely to win a game** (but it means you didn't really win).

It can make adults think you're better at doing things than you are.

It can make it **easy to get all your work right**.

It can **seem easier to cheat** than to do things properly (but it will **stop you from learning**).

...Or playing fairly

Most children know playing fairly is the right thing to do, even if they don't always do it! Here's why it's a good idea not to cheat...

Everyone prefers to play with a friend who plays fairly.

I'll play with you.

If you never cheat, doing well is a real achievement and you can feel proud of yourself.

SPELLING CHAMPION

You really deserve that.

It's good to be someone people can trust.

I'm just getting a drink of water. I trust you not to look.

It's always more satisfying to do things properly, instead of cheating.

I didn't get my older brother to make it this time.

It's good to know...
People who don't cheat understand that joining in, having fun and playing fairly feels much better than always winning or being right.

13

Being bossy...

Some people are naturally bossier than others. Being bossy is about telling your friends what to do and not thinking about what they might like to do instead. Why do some people think that being bossy is a good idea?

You get to do exactly **what you want.**

It can **save time** if people just do what they're told.

You can make sure things are done **the way you want them done.**

You might always be the person **in charge** and that might feel good.

...Or listening to others

It's much better to listen to others and find out what everyone wants to do, rather than just being bossy.

It's kind to listen to others and they will like it when you do.

Other people have good ideas too and these ideas can make things **even better**.

If more than one person is involved in making a decision, it's **usually better**.

You can **relax** a bit when you're not always in charge.

It's good to know...

When someone is being bossy, they often don't see why it's a problem. It's good to tell them how they're making you feel, so they understand why it's not always the best way to behave.

Saying mean things...

Saying unkind things to other people is never helpful. It makes everyone feel uncomfortable and can hurt people's feelings. Why do we sometimes say mean things?

We might be mean because we're **jealous** of someone.

Great save!

You're still a terrible goalie.

Maybe we haven't learnt that being kind is a better way to behave.

You can't play because nobody likes you.

We might say mean things to make **others laugh.**

Look at his knees – he looks like a hippo.

We might be in a **bad mood** and finding it hard to be kind.

Your sandwiches stink.

...Or being kind

It's really good to get into the habit of saying kind things to people, and being nice feels much better for everyone than being mean. What's great about being kind?

If you show kindness to others, you are more likely to get kindness in return.

If you show kindness to others, you are more likely to get kindness in return.

Saying kind things always cheers people up.

People will know you are a **nice person**.

Being kind can make you feel closer to other people.

It's good to know...
It's very easy to be kind with your words. Sometimes, it only takes a few words to make someone else really happy.

Giving Up...

When we find something difficult to do, or if success doesn't come easily, we may decide to just give up. Why do we sometimes give up?

It can seem **much easier to give up** than to stick with something.

It's too hard, I give up.

We might give up because we're **frustrated**.

It's so frustrating. I'm never going to work out how to ride it!

When we give up, it means we can **get on** with something we find easier.

If we give up trying harder things and stick to easier things, it feels like **we're good at everything** and we might like that.

I'm good at cooking, football and jigsaw puzzles. I won't try anything else.

...Or being determined

Determination is when we keep trying until we succeed or get really good at something. It takes more time, effort and focus than giving up. It's good to be determined because...

Determination means we are more likely to get good at things.

Being determined is a quality that makes us stand out.

It's much **more satisfying being good at** something we found difficult at first.

Many **great achievements** are down to determination.

It's good to know...
People often give up because they don't like finding something difficult. It's very brave to stick at something we don't find easy, and it takes patience.

Doing things that aren't good for you...

People do lots of things that they know aren't good for them like eating too many sweets, not exercising, not getting enough sleep or not doing their homework. Why are we tempted to do these things?

Things that are not good for us can be fun at the time (like staying up late!).

We often copy what other people do **without** thinking about whether it's good or bad for us.

Things that are not good for us are often extremely tempting.

Sometimes we just feel lazy and don't make the best choices.

Maybe I'll start later.

TO DO
Homework ☐
Exercise ☐
Chores ☐

...Or being good to yourself

Doing plenty of exercise, taking time to relax, eating fruit and vegetables, drinking lots of water, getting enough sleep and learning new things are all good for us. It's not always easy to do all of these things, but let's take a look at why they are great.

Eating food that is good for us means we are **less likely to get ill.**

Delicious!

Learning new things is always **interesting.**

Things that are good for us can also be **fun.**

We can feel **proud** when we've been good to ourselves.

SUPER STAR

It's good to know...
Of course, everyone can have treats now and then as a nice reward!

Rushing to get things done...

Sometimes children rush jobs they are given to do or they rush their work at school. Why might rushing seem like a good idea?

It gets the job out of the way quickly.

We might be encouraged to do things quickly.

We can get on with things we enjoy more once the job is done.

We might not see the importance of doing a job properly.

...Or doing things carefully

Although it's tempting to rush to get jobs done, it's usually much better if we take our time. Let's think about why this is.

Taking our time means we're more likely to do our best.

It took me ages.

If we take our time, we usually enjoy a job more.

I've carefully sorted the buttons. It was very satisfying.

Taking care to do a job well can be relaxing.

Doing a job carefully usually means we'll notice and learn more.

Hmm, that's interesting!

It's good to know...

It's best to take your time and do a job well, but it's also possible to take too long to do a job – especially if you take too long because you're not really focused on it!

23

Staying cross with someone...

We can stay cross with friends when they do something that upsets us and we don't manage to sort it out. When we are cross with someone we might moan about them, sulk or decide not to speak to them. Why might we stay cross with a friend?

It can be **easier to be cross, sulk or moan** than to sort things out.

It can sometimes make us **feel connected** with others if we are all cross together.

We might think it's **too hard to talk** to the person and sort things out.

We might think it's **up to the other person** to sort out the situation.

...Or forgiving them

Forgiving someone is nearly always a good idea. Let's have a look at why this is.

If we forgive, we are more likely to sort things out.

We all make mistakes, so it's good to know that we can all be forgiven.

Forgiving people always makes us feel better in the end.

Forgiving someone means they no longer have a bad effect on us.

It's good to know...

If someone upsets you, it's best to let them know. Your goal is for everyone to feel better, and this usually involves talking to the person and finding forgiveness.

25

Boasting...

Boasting is when you tell other people how great you are – a lot! Sometimes what you boast about is true and sometimes it's exaggerated. Boasting means you don't talk about the things you're not so good at. Why do people boast?

Boasting can make you the **centre of attention.**

> I've climbed the tallest mountain in the world.

It can feel great to talk about your best bits and not about the things you find hard.

> I've never got anything wrong in maths.

You might boast to **insist people notice** your achievements.

> I caught a fish three times the size of me.

Boasting can be a way of telling other people that you think you're **better than them.**

> I won the race... again! I'm the fastest runner in the class.

...Or being modest

Being modest is when you get on with things and never boast about yourself. Why is being modest a good thing?

You never make others feel bad about things they cannot do or haven't done.

Being modest is **impressive** in itself.

Wow, I didn't know you'd won! You're so modest.

It helps you understand that **everyone's** achievements are special.

It means you don't need others to notice what you've done to be happy.

Your picture is great.

It's good to know...
It's good to be pleased about your skills and achievements, but always talking about them can make others feel bad. We all have things we're good at and not so good at.

Being grumpy...

Everyone feels grumpy now and then but it's best to keep your grumpiness to yourself, as grumpiness can spread! Why might people be grumpy?

It's a quick way to make others **leave you alone.**

Go away! I'm really cross.

You might not think about **the effect** your behaviour has on other people.

You might just **be tired, hungry, thirsty** or hot.

Some days when lots of bad things happen, your **grumpiness builds up and bursts out.**

...Or being cheerful

You can't always be cheerful, but when you are it's great because...

You're more likely to say kind things.

People want to spend time with you.

Being cheerful towards others makes them feel respected.

Being cheerful spreads from person to person.

It's good to know...

Everyone feels grumpy sometimes. This isn't a problem unless you take it out on other people. When you're feeling cheerful, it's great to spread it about. You could even cheer up a whole room!

Notes for grown-ups

Behaviour (or the actions we take) is usually due to one of the following:

- to fulfil a basic need like eating food or keeping warm
- to get attention
- to get something we want
- to get away from others
- to avoid a demand.

For very young children, who have a small vocabulary, behaviour is often their most effective way of communicating. As we know, this can sometimes result in quite extreme behaviours that can be difficult to manage. However, as children get a bit older and their vocabulary, understanding and ability to empathise increase, they can begin to consider their behaviour more consciously. This is where this book comes in!

By sharing this book with your child, you can help them consider why they might behave in certain ways, the impact their behaviour has on others and some alternative ways of behaving in different situations. This process could help your child develop empathy, make connections between behaviour and emotions, think about habitual behaviours and ultimately make more conscious decisions about how they behave.

Advice for younger children

Catch your child getting things right
Young children sometimes crave attention but all too often they get it mostly when they're misbehaving. When an adult praises a child for making good choices and behaving well, the attention that their good behaviour gets will make them more likely to behave well in future. Try praising your child for everyday things like sitting sensibly at the table, showing kindness to a sibling or going to bed without making a fuss. You could explain to your child why these behaviours are so helpful and the effect they have on you and others.

Link emotions to behaviour
Help your child to see that although their emotions can have an impact on their behaviour, they always have a choice about how to behave – even when they're really angry. Help your child to regularly focus on their emotions and work out what emotion they're feeling and where in their body they're feeling it. This can help to separate the emotion from the resulting behaviour. This approach takes practice but should help your child not to react in the heat of the moment (when rational thinking is reduced and impulsive behaviours are more likely) and instead make a more positive choice about the best response when an uncomfortable feeling arises.

Tell a story

If your child often engages in a particularly unhelpful behaviour, you could make up a story about another child who does exactly the same thing. Talk about the make-believe child and ask your child to comment on their behaviour. This can not only give insights and open up conversations about what is going on for your child when they behave this way, but they might even offer solutions for the fictitious child that they can apply to themselves.

Take time to reflect

When your child has behaved in an unhelpful way, speculate about why they might have done so. Try starting with the phrase, 'I wonder if you…'. For example, 'I wonder if you pushed your brother because I was busy and didn't answer your question and you wanted my attention'. This can help your child link their behaviour to their thoughts and needs. It doesn't matter if your speculation is right or wrong, it's more important that there is some reflection upon what happened, why it happened, and what action would have been more helpful.

Be a role model

Parents and carers are usually the main influencers in a child's life. None of us are perfect, but it's important that we demonstrate the ability to reflect on what we've done, apologise when we make mistakes and think about what behaviour might have been more effective in any situation.

Talk about the best and worse

At bedtime, have a brief conversation with your child about the best and the worst parts of the day. Start with the worst and see if they can explain what their underlying feelings

were, what happened, how they responded, what anyone else involved might have been feeling, what they could have done differently and so on. Then, end on a good note by exploring the best parts and how your child felt about them.

Advice for older children

Help your child to empathise

Help your child to consider the impact their behaviour has on others by imagining how they would feel if someone was behaving the same way towards them. Some children are naturally better at this than others but all children can learn to do this.

Teach your child to understand what a habit is

Lots of behaviours – some healthy and some not so healthy – are habits. Most people engage in habits and they can be hard to break.

To help children change a habit, we need to:

- Encourage them to think about why a habit is unhelpful and what the benefits of stopping it would be.

- Get them to consider how they want to define themselves in term of habits, e.g. 'Do I want to be a lazy person or a person who exercises regularly?' This can help motivate them as they can link habits to their desired identity.

- Teach them to anticipate the moments when resisting a helpful habit or engaging in an unhelpful habit might tempt them most, and find alternative actions.

- Make it more difficult for them to access unhelpful habits (e.g. don't put the biscuit tin within their reach) or make it easier to access healthy habits (e.g. put the fruit bowl within their reach).

- Support each other in the process of stopping an unhelpful habit when possible. If you and your child decide to engage in a healthy habit, support each other to do so by doing it together. Plan rewards for when you achieve the new habit.

Encourage motivation

An extremely valuable life skill we can help children develop is being motivated to achieve goals. Find opportunities to teach your child how to be motivated when they show an interest in achieving something. Start by setting a goal, then break it down into what it would look like each day or week. Discuss what could prevent their goal from being achieved and how to overcome these hurdles. Praise them when they achieve a goal and encourage them to continue.

Think about values

Our values affect how we behave. For example, if we feel fairness is a value that should be respected, we will try to ensure that fairness is an outcome in our interactions. Other values that can be beneficial to behaviour include tolerance, forgiveness, honesty, taking responsibility for our actions, respect, compassion, loyalty, generosity, gratitude, etc. You could discuss the benefits of different values and the impact they might have on behaviour with your child as they get older.

Finally...

Children nearly always find it easier to follow positive instructions rather than negative ones. Instead of saying, 'Don't mess about', you could say, 'I need you to sit quietly for a few minutes'. Try to keep the language you use to guide children's behaviour positive and specific.